W.L. ASTOR

FINANCIALLY FORWAR

**The Ultimate Guide on How to Make Money During
Recession, Learn the Effective Strategies on How You Can
Take Advantage of Recession and Make Tons of Money**

Descrierea CIP a Bibliotecii Naţionale a României
W.L. ASTOR
    **FINANCIALLY FORWAR. The Ultimate Guide on How to
Make Money During Recession, Learn the Effective Strategies
on How You Can Take Advantage of Recession and Make Tons
of Money** / W.L. Astor – Bucharest: Editura My Ebook, 2021
    ISBN

W.L. ASTOR

FINANCIALLY FORWAR

The Ultimate Guide on How to Make Money During Recession, Learn the Effective Strategies on How You Can Take Advantage of Recession and Make Tons of Money

My Ebook Publishing House
Bucharest, 2021

W. L. ASTON

FINANCIALLY FORWARD

The Ultimate Guide on How to Make Money During Recession. Learn the Effective Strategies on How You Can Take Advantage of Recession and Make Tons of Money

My Book Publishing House
Bucharest 2021

TABLE OF CONTENTS

FOREWORD

The financial gurus will be arguing for years how we got into the economic mess we're in - and just how we'll get out of it. But while all the babbling and blaming is going on, you'd like to know how to prop up your resources so you won't have to worry about every little dip in the economy.

Here are tried and true techniques you are able to master - how to spend less, reduce your debt and muck more. Center on what you are able to control. Small steps can truly make a big difference.

Recession Retribution

How To Fight Back During A Recession And Save Your Financial Future!

CHAPTER 1

YOU NEED TO SAVE

Synopsis

Saving money may be a true challenge when your budget is tight – an unforeseen expense here, another there; and oops there's no income left to save. If you're sick of having to dodge saving, then this is for you!

Put Some Away

Keep saving easy by taking yourself out of the equation. Utilize your bank's auto-draft feature to schedule steady transfers from your checking account to your savings account. Then, take it easy; and let the bank manage all of the particulars for you.

Did you get a raise at work? Try not to consider it as an opportunity to super-size your life-style, but a chance to super-size your savings. Step-up your 401(k) savings by the sum of your raise, or use your auto-draft to put the extra money in savings. Then, continue on with your current lifestyle.

Accessible income is money that's likely to get spent up. Keep your savings unreachable by sticking it at a different bank than your checking account. The additional hassle of going to another bank will make you think twice about using it. CDs and savings bonds are likewise good savings tools for keeping money out of view.

Saving change is in no way a fresh idea, but there's a reason for that: it actually works. Make a habit of putting all of your change into a jar each night. Then, put the money into a savings account when the jar is full.

To hike up your savings even more, make a game out of searching for coins in parking areas. It's even more amusing to save, when you're saving somebody else's money.

Do you take part in a lot of rebate offers? If so, think about sticking all of your rebate checks into a savings account. You aren't in all likelihood going to miss the money, but you're likely to like getting those savings statements in the mail.

Illness, job loss, house repairs, auto repairs - there are so many matters that may rock your financial ship. Are you organized to address them? Begin an emergency fund, and you won't have to question.

Determine how much you'd like to put away. A thousand, 3 to 6 month's living expenses, a year's wages. There many opinions out there about how much income you should place into an emergency fund, but the only view that matters is yours. Ask yourself how much you'd need to have put away to feel safe, and make that the amount that you lay aside in your emergency fund.

Establish a list of all of your steady monthly expenses, housing costs, food, utilities, debt repayments, transit costs, insurance and all of your other "must-pay" bills. Then, total your every month expenses, and multiply the resulting figure by the number of month's that you decided to put away. For instance, if you need to cover $2,500 in every month expenses for 3 months, you'll need to allow for $7,500 in your emergency fund.

Once you've ascertained how much you need to save, it's time to choose where you'll keep your money. Because you want your emergency fund to stay fairly accessible, a savings account, money market account or short-run CD make common sense.

Any one of these accounts will provide you the liquidness that you need, while still bringing in some interest.

If you're like most individuals, it's going to take time to develop your emergency fund, likely even a lot of time. That's all right. The crucial thing is that you get moving now. Look over your finances, and ascertain how much you are able to afford to put toward your emergency fund monthly.

Even a little will help, so don't worry if that's all you are able to afford to do.

Turn a creative eye on your finances, and you're sure to discover ways to reach your savings goal quicker.

CHAPTER 2

CUT DOWN SPENDING

Synopsis

Postpone or do away with unneeded purchases. Then, add the savings to your emergency fund.

Spend Wisely

Cutting down on your spending does not have to mean lots of giving up of things. Try out a few of these painless cost-cutters, and observe your spending reduce to a more comfortable level.

Fancy Name brand products are great, but regular store brand products are frequently even as good (if not one in the same). Make the change over to the bargain labels, and you will shave twenty-five to fifty percent off of your weekly grocery store bill. With increasingly more grocery store chains bringing out their own line of organics and additional premium products, there's never been a more comfortable time to shift.

Have you ever gone to the store for a couple of particulars and emerged with a whole trunk full of things? Who hasn't? To prevent impulse shopping from grabbing your budget, make a habit of shopping with a list. Write down everything you need, and then merely shop for those items. You might be still enticed to add an extra item to your cart. Head home and consider it first. If you still need the item you are able to always add it to your next shopping list.

Dining out always costs more than dining at home – whether it's a speedy snack from a convenience store, a vending machine or a fast food place. Prevent this cost altogether by keeping snacks on hand at all times. Put a granola bar and a bottle of some sort of beverage in your purse or satchel before running errands; squirrel away some goodies in your desk drawer at work - just be prepared for that hunger attack where and if it decides to come up.

Whether it's food in your pantry, hobby provisions or beauty care merchandise, you likely have lots of unused or partially utilized items around your home. Before you dash out to the store to purchase your next "must-have," look around and see if you are able to find something at home to fill your requirement. This easy exercise won't only help you to spend to a lesser extent, but likewise to clean out some of the clutter in your house.

Challenge yourself to save more every time you go out to shop. If you generally purchase something at regular price, challenge yourself to discover it on sale. If you generally purchase something on sale, challenge yourself to discover it on clearance. When you're forever on the lookout for a deal, there's no end to the money that you are able to save; and before long it becomes a game that you look forward to acting on.

CHAPTER 3

PAY DEBT

Synopsis

A recession is not all sorry news. Since rates of interest tend to go down during recessive periods, your debts will cost you less; and your debt repayment dollars will go farther. It's a good time to pay down charge card debt.

Look over your budget, and ascertain if you are able to afford to use more money to pay off your debt.

Likewise keep an eye on the mortgage rates. Now may be the time to refinance to a lower interest rate and a shorter mortgage term.

Pay It Off

To pay off your debt, you need to:

1. Evaluate Your Debt
2. Produce a Budget
3. Cut down Your Spending
4. Begin Saving
5. Attack Your Debt

If you are ready to put your debts to rest once and for all and truly begin paying it down, Here are some ideas to bring in some extra cash to put toward your debt reduction efforts:

➢ You are able to have a garage sale.

Extra debris around the house is income just waiting to be liquefied. Gather up all of your old clothes, playthings, house wares, and pieces of furniture, and have a garage sale. Then put the money you make toward your debt of choice. If you have valuable items to sell- think about listing them on EBay or in the classified section of your local paper.

➢ As we discussed before you are able to save your change.

Do you have a change jar? If you don't... get one. If you do, it's time to get into it. Roll all of your coins, and then make an additional debt payment equal to the amount that you've rolled up. Duplicate the process every time your jar is full.

➢ You are able to use coupons.

Using coupons is a good way to save money on the things that you require, however it may likewise be a great way to advance your debt repayment attempts. Challenge yourself to utilize as many coupons as you are able to when you grocery shop, and then repay your efforts by placing the money saved toward your debt.

➢ You are able to hire yourself.

Do you employ somebody to cut your grass or clean your home? If so, it might be time to hire yourself for the task. Take on a couple of the tasks that you'd commonly hire somebody else to do, and then "pay yourself" by putting the savings towards your debt.

➢ You are able to share your views.

Do you have views? Turn them into a paycheck by signing on for paid online surveys. You are able to complete as many or as few as you've time for, and then put the money toward paying off a debt early.

➢ You are able to turn cash gifts into payments.

Do you have a relative that likes to send you money as a gift? Then pass that gift on to one of your credit cards, and watch your account balance come down.

➢ You are able to cash in on a talent.

Hobbies are commonly a source of spending, but that doesn't have to be the norm. Establish a list of all of the things that you're good at, and then brainstorm ways to turn them into a reservoir of revenue. Can you give knitting lessons? Hire yourself out as a painter? Become a part-time landscape gardener? Discover a way to promote your skill or skills, and then turn your earnings into payments.

> You are able to bank your bonuses.

We all profit from the occasional bonanza, whether it's a work bonus, an income tax return or something else totally. Vow to turn your bonus income into bonus debt repayments, and wring your hands over those credit card statements a bit less.

CHAPTER 4

PUT STUFF IN RESERVE

Synopsis

Prices may be a bit irregular during a recession. The resolution? Establish a reserve of sale-priced foods and commodities, and you'll only have to purchase when it's a good deal for you.

Pile It Up

Stockpiling is a basic practice among frugal people and for good cause: it may save a ton. If you're sick of paying full price for your foodstuffs, it might be time to begin a stockpile of your own. Here's how it works:

- Assemble a list of all the items that you utilize on a steady basis (food and differently). Make sure to include toiletries, paper products, cleansers and pet provisions (if needed).

- List the particulars on your stockpile list in a notebook, and start tracking how much you pay for them. Take exceptional care to notice any sales that you chance upon, along with the date of the sale and the name of the store where you discovered it.

- After a couple of months, your price book will show a good deal of valuable info, including what you commonly pay for things, which store has the better price on each item on your list and even how often particular sales happen.

- A stockpile only saves money when it bears particulars that have been bought on sale or gotten free of charge, so don't anticipate that you'll construct a huge stockpile overnight. Center your efforts on discovering those too-good-to-pass-up sales, and the stockpile will take form on its own:

  ➤ Try to spot the sale leaders in the weekly sales circulars
  ➤ Clip coupons, and correspond them to sales

➤ Blend manufacturer coupons and store coupons to maximize your savings

➤ Capitalize on rebate offers

➤ Snap up clearance items

Stockpiling is easy to exaggerate. Before you go crazy and purchase eighty-nine tubes of toothpaste, spend some time measuring your actual needs. Some stockpilers purchase enough of a particular to get to the next sale, while other people want to purchase enough to get through a particular number of months. Whichever technique you pick, it's crucial to keep expiration dates in mind. You won't save any money by purchasing more than you are able to use:

As your stockpiling skills better, you're going to start to uncover more gratis and nearly-free deals. A little of advice from a veteran stockpiler: only stockpile things that you'll really utilize. If your loved ones didn't eat a certain brand of cereal when you purchased it at full-price, they won't eat it when you get it free of charge either.

Once those deals start to amass, you'll need to discover a way to organize them. 1st step: assigning a spot in your house for your stockpile. Pantries and cellars are good – if you've got them – However guest room closets, empty drawers and even that space under your bed will work.

Think creatively, and you'll discover the perfect spot for your stockpile.

Then, your only challenge will be maintaining your stockpile in a neat and orderly way. A couple of ideas to get you going:

➤ Put like items together

➤ Revolve your stock, pushing fresh items to the back and moving aged items to the front

➤ Freeze flour before stashing away to avoid bug infestations

CHAPTER 5

MAKE DO

Synopsis

No need to purchase new when you are able to make do. Consume leftovers; discover substitutes for items that you've run out of; find new uses for the things that you already have; and you'll keep that shopping list withering month after month.

Use What You Have

Has a great sale or harvest left you with more food than you are able to utilize now? No need to let it go to waste. Here are directions for freezing a few foods you might have never entertained freezing:

➢ Eggs

Combine the yolks and egg whites collectively, and pour into an ice cube tray. 2 cubes are equal to one large egg.

➢ Milk

Keep it in its original container, but take out enough milk to allow for expansion – around 1 cup per gallon of milk.

Defrost in the refrigerator, and shake well prior to using.

➢ Butter

Keep it in its original container. Defrost in the refrigerator to utilize.

➢ Bananas

Freeze in the peel. Then, merely thaw and peel to utilize in smoothies and breads. Note: the peel will turn dark, but that won't affect the caliber of the banana in the least.

➢ Celery

Wash and cut to wanted size. Then, quick-freeze on a tray, and transfer to a freezer bag or a different airtight container.

To utilize: add the frozen celery directly to soups or other hot dishes.

➢ Tomatoes

Wash well. Then, freeze whole and unpeeled on a tray. Put in freezer bags once totally frozen.

➢ Fresh Herbs

Cut finely. Then, put in an ice cube tray along with a small bit of water. To utilize: merely drop frozen cubes directly into hot dishes.

➢ Nuts

Freeze (either in shell or shelled) in a deep-freeze bag or another airtight container.

➢ Zucchini and Other Squash

Wash and chop to wanted size. Then, blanch for 3 minutes; let cool; and freeze in an airtight container.

➢ Apples

Freeze whole or chopped up, peeled or unpeeled.

Vinegar can be utilized to clean your house, to make health and beauty products, to do away with pests and more.

Vinegar makes stain removal a snap. Here are some ideas using white vinegar and a bit of effort.

➢ Tomato Stains

Saturate the stain with vinegar. Let it soak in. Then, launder.

➢ Sugar-Based Stains

Saturate the stain with vinegar. Let it soak in. Then, launder.

➤ Coffee/ Tea Stains

Flush the area with vinegar to withdraw the stain. Rinse off and repeat as required. Then, launder as usual.

➤ Wine Stains

Saturate the stain with vinegar, and let it stand for numerous minutes. Then, rinse off with water, and duplicate the process, if required. Launder right away after.

➤ Mustard Stains

Put vinegar on the stain, and let it soak in. Then, spot treat with a little laundry detergent, and launder.

➤ Grease

Soak the stain in pure white vinegar. Then, launder as usual.

➤ Sweat Stains

Pour vinegar over the sweat stain. Then rub coarse salt into the stain (common salt will work if it's all you have). Put the garment out in the sun to dry. Then, launder.

➤ Grass Stains

Put vinegar on the stain with a sponge, and gently dab to lift. If the stain remains, make a spread of vinegar and baking soda, and brush it into the stain with an old toothbrush. Then, launder as usual.

➤ Ink Stains

Apply vinegar to the stain. Then, rub with a spread made of vinegar and baking soda. Let dry. Then, launder.

➤ Deodorant Stains

Rub vinegar into the stain till it disappears. Then, launder as usual.

CHAPTER 6

MAKE IT LAST LONGER

Synopsis

Pinch more life out of everything that you own, and you won't have to pinch as much income out of your budget for replacement items.

Squeeze More Out

Sick of replacing razor blades, printer cartridges and additional household necessities every time you turn around? Here's how to make some of those items last longer:

➤ **Shampoo and Conditioner**

Store bottles inverted to keep the shampoo or conditioner from bogging down at the bottom of the bottle. When you can't get any more out, add a couple of capfuls of water, and shake.

➤ Toothpaste

Once you've forced out as much toothpaste as you are able to, cut the tube open with a scissors, and you'll have enough for a lot more brushings. Store the cut tube in a plastic bag between uses to avoid dry out.

➤ Razors

Dry the blades off following every use, and they'll remain sharp longer.

➤ Shower Gel

Put your shower gel on a loofah, rather than on your skin, and a little squirt will bring forth endless lather.

➤ Lipstick

When you arrive at the bottom of a tube, use a lip brush or a Q-tip to get to the left over lipstick. Put your lipstick leftovers into an empty lip gloss pot for easy on the go utilization.

➤ Bar Soap

Undo your soap and let it dry for a couple weeks before you use it. How come? Because dry soap does not dissolve as quickly when it comes into contact with water.

➤ Laundry Detergent

More detergent does not mean fresher clothes; it just means more soap residual on your clothes. Try utilizing half as much detergent as the manufacturer advocates, and you probably won't even notice the difference.

➤ Spray Cleaners

Set the spray nozzle to the lowest mist setting. Less emerging means less being utilized.

➤ Clothing

What's an easy way to stretch the life of all your clothes? Omit the dryer. All that heat just is not good for your clothes.

> **Shoes**

Remove dirt and scuff marks off of your shoes as soon as you observe them to avoid any permanent harm.

> **Food**

Food spoilage is frequently the result of unsuitable storage. Learn how to store the foods that you eat on a regular basis.

> **Candles**

Put candles in the freezer for a few hours before you utilize them. This will cause the wax to burn slower and more equally.

> **Mattresses**

Follow the manufacturer's ideas for flipping and rotating your mattress to avoid premature sagging.

> **Refrigerators**

Vacuum the condenser coil every 3 months (once monthly if you have animals).

➤ Markers

Renovate dried out markers by stashing away vertically (tip down) for a day or two. If that does not work, try dipping the tips in alcohol for a couple of minutes.

CHAPTER 7

MAKE SURE YOU KEEP YOUR INCOME

Synopsis

The most important thing you want to do is protect your income.

Be Prepared

If you work for or own a company that's going to feel very little issues as a result of a recession you've very little to worry about. Irrespective of what company you work for, all the same, now is a capital time to begin making yourself indispensable. It's simple fact that the employees that are the 1st to go when lay-offs happen are the ones who aren't viewed as crucial enough to stay.

Making yourself an indispensable part of your company is the opening move making sure you maintain your income. Even companies that are cutting back their staff are going to pause with persons who are crucial to their company's daily operations.

If you are able to, involve yourself in many projects your company is working on (plainly without stretching yourself so thin that you're no longer able to do a good job). The more things you have your fingers in, the harder it will be to let you go. In times of recession companies might be cutting down on their employees, but that doesn't mean that they're going to be able to cut down on the amount of work they have to do. It simply means that that work is going to be re-delegated. If you're already actively involved in a lot of projects the company will feel it much easier to give you extra duties on these projects than to try to bring a fresh man up to speed.

This isn't the time to try to apply for a promotion or a transfer. The moment you accept this type of move you get to be the new man on the totem pole, and directly become more vulnerable when the time arrives to go through and choose who will go and who will stay.

Mental attitude counts. When companies are attempting to decide who will stay and who will go, often mental attitude and the employee's ability to boost team spirit is as strong a determiner as their ability to do their job. Remember, companies attempting to stay on top during a recession are going to have greater expectations of their employees than ever before. The only way these employees are going to be able to fulfill those expectations is if they're able to keep their morale high.

Hopefully the economic recession isn't going to impact your income stream-but that doesn't mean you shouldn't take safeguards.

It's all about networking. If you've remained in touch with your bosses and associates, both past and current, you'll not only likely already know who's hiring and who's not; you might have the inside track when it comes to finding another job.

If you wait to connect with them till you've been laid off, however, you're going to discover yourself scrambling.

They're going to know that the only reason you're getting hold of them is because you're hoping to acquire a job, and they're going to view you unfavorably.

Regardless how much you've been looking ahead to spending the next 3 weeks on vacation, when your company begins making budget cuts is utterly, positively not the time to take an long vacation. You can't show somebody how useful you are if you're not there!

That doesn't mean you have to strip yourself of a well earned workweek away from the office. If you tend to take your vacations in mass (disappearing for 2 to 3 weeks at a time) this is a good opportunity to spread those vacations out a little. No one expects you to work yourself to your demise.

CHAPTER 8

CREATE ANOTHER INCOME STREAM

Synopsis

Produce another income stream, even a little one. Perhaps you take a second job for a month to pay off a credit card or perhaps you sell your baseball cards on EBay or perhaps you find another way to begin a small business on the side.

A Little Extra

As the economic system moves closer and closer to a worse situation, we've seen many layoffs happening. How do you protect yourself and make sure you have a little extra coming in?

Companies aren't hiring, have started process improvement efforts and are viewing ways to cut costs by delaying equipment and software upgrades.

Getting laid off in a beneficial economy isn't as big of a deal as when the economy is in a recession. Occasionally it even pays to get off the ship before it sinks. If you've a good chance of getting laid off in the next year, you may prefer to consider finding another job while you still have a job. That way, you are able to move to the next job with minimum income loss.

The most beneficial way to avoid a layoff is to have your own clients. The one thing that I disfavor the most about working for somebody else is that when you leave – they keep the clients. The clients are the gems of any company, furnishing the revenue to pay the expenses and the employees. When push comes to shove, employees are let go, but the owners keep the clients that the employees have worked hard to acquire. Business owners don't get fired, although they may go bankrupt if they get too far in debt.

I'm not advising you give up your day job and begin a business – at any rate not before you've done your homework. Beginning a business takes a lot of work, patience, money and a rare amount of ambition. Most individuals only succeed after bombing several times.

What I am advising is that you consider setting up the basis of a small side business. You may begin your business as a hobby and slowly begin adding clients. If you get fired, you'd have the basis all setup and a small client base already in place. This gives you the choice of either returning to find a different job or centering on your small business for income. A small business may be your insurance – reducing your risk of a fiscal hardship.

Drastic changes in the economic system will push a lot of businesses into bankruptcy and fresh products and services will be needed that weren't needed a short time ago. For instance, the need for foreclosure info and counselors has skyrockets in just the last six months. A lot of individuals will be seeking fresh ways to live with the changes all around them. If you're seeking business ideas, I'd look at the needs of a recession economy. Your most beneficial protection from a layoff is to get your own clients.

CHAPTER 9

CONSIDER YOUR HOME

Synopsis

Your mortgage payment is probably your biggest monthly bill. Reduce your mortgage with one of the many options including downsizing, doubling up, renting, refinancing or even foreclosing.

Consider Options

Assuming you can't sell your home... here are some ideas

If you purchased your home with 0% down and it's worth less than your real estate loan, then your most beneficial option is to just foreclose. You've nothing to lose but your credit – which will be repaired with time anyhow. But, if you've a significant sum of money in your home, then foreclosing is a much more difficult choice – and in this case you need to consider your long term financial outlook. If you're likely to lose your job in the following few years, then you ought to think about foreclosure now instead of sometime in the future. There are lots of houses for rent and the cost of renting is really low because of the many houses that are not selling, so you'll find another place to live. If you're planning to foreclose, call your lender after a couple of months of missing payments and ask for a non- recourse foreclosure, which entails the bank accepting the house as full payment and provides up their right to try to get any more money from you in the time to come. (You should refer to a licensed pro before making any of these conclusions)

If you wait it out, all mortgage lenders are sooner or later going to be in very hard positions. Sooner or later your lender will be forced to do whatever they may to keep you from foreclosing, even if it means forgiving 50% of your loan worth. Life isn't fair, and it's not going to be fair when the cat next to you gets his mortgage cut in half while you yielded full price. If your lender won't shift, then ask to refinance at a lower fixed rate. If your lender still won't shift, as most lenders are only talking terms with delinquent borrowers, try not paying your mortgage for a couple of months and then ask again.

If the home is your primary residence, think about renting a room to a university student. If there's a college in your area, just put up circulars on the college bulletin boards advertising your room for rent – accenting the many rewards of living in a house vs. a dormitory.

How about a college exchange student? Telephone your local college and ask about their exchange student plan. College exchange students are students from other nations that visit the US by attending a US college. You are able to likewise try finding a niece or nephew in your family tree that would like to try living on their own. This idea is particularly enticing if you live in a distant place from your niece or nephew for of the added adventure of traveling to a new place and experiencing new things.

You are able to also market the advantages of living in a house to apartment renters, by placing flyers on apartments in your area. You are able to offer advantages like, a garage, a yard with a nearby park, an individual entry or allowing pets. There are a lot of individuals in apartments that would love to enjoy some of the advantages of home owners.

Find another family to live with you and partake in the costs of your home. This works great if you've a house that's naturally separated like a rambler with a finished basement as it gives each family the privacy they require. The kids will likely love the idea of more kids to play with and if you're lucky one of your kids can sit for both families from time to time. This thought can likewise cut the chores in half as both families help to sustain the house. To discover a great family to double up with, just ask around your acquaintances, family, church or other social groups that you're involved in.

Leverage your home as office space to begin a home business. Utilize an extra room for your home office. Your home business wouldn't have to use up all your spare time, just enough to help you pay your mortgage. I advise that you begin very small. The Net is among the best places to seek home businesses. You may try selling things on eBay.com or affiliate marketing or any number of things.

You may likewise call a few local businesses and ask if there's anything you are able to help them with from your home office, like accounting or letter writing or dictation or anything else.

A small income from a home business may be just enough to keep you out front of your mortgage payments, and you are able to leverage the office space of your home to get it. A home business is likewise a good tax shelter.

CHAPTER 10

CONSIDER INVESTMENTS

Synopsis

Move your investments to lower-risk securities like bonds during the market shakedown, than move back to stocks after the market hits the bottom – in a couple of years. A different option is to invest in commodities like gold, silver, wheat and corn, which are bringing back high profits, but they're also very risks, so be heedful and don't bet the farm.

Moving Money

The drastic market conditions have taken quite a chunk out of many 401k balances this year.

The biggest headache is that the dollar is replaced as the worlds Reserve Currency with the Euro or Yen or several other currencies or combinations. The dollar is seesawing on collapse as the world is draining of willingness to continue to lend money to us as the global financial crisis is reversing their investments in dollars.

We may choose to brush aside the evidence against the dollar all we want, but sooner or later the evidence will demand a finding of fact. Here are a few other reasons that the world may face a dollar currency crisis very soon.

In light of this economic assessment, we might want to move money out of the bond market prior to the dollar dropping anymore. Sure, bonds are dependable if you just want to conserve your dollars, but most of us don't want our dollars back after they have lost ninety percent of their worth. I likewise think many of the foreign markets are over sold from the rush to the bond market with little regard for the company's earnings. When the dollar drops, rising prices will come back with a vengeance and that will drive up the prices of trade goods – particularly gold.

Stay alert as to what is going on in the financial industry. A recession may shake things up very fast, causing old industries to collapse (like the housing market) and fresh industries to be born (like the alternative energy market).

The data you gain may save you a lot of money and lead you to fresh opportunities. Make it part of your day-to-day routine to read a couple of articles every day and a couple of books each year. Being prepared for opportunities is maybe the best technique you are able to have. The individuals who are out of debt and stay informed, may stumble upon a once in a lifetime opportunity.

I'm not a licensed financial advisor, so please confer with a licensed professional before making any investing or financial decision.

WRAPPING UP

We're frequently told that the current financial meltdown is the most grievous since the Great Depression. And while that might be true, comparing today's times to such a dreadful and demoralizing crisis has the effect of frightening people, thereby making the situation worse. This is the incorrect way to react to the situation. Instead of passively absorbing fear and uncertainty, we would do well to remember that some individuals managed to stay afloat during the Great Depression. In that way, hopefully this book has given you some money saving tips and ways to secure your financial future.

9 786069 838105

Printed by Libri Plureos GmbH in Hamburg, Germany